Alice in The Wonderland

Themed Cookbook

A List of Magical Recipes of Meals and Drinks in The Wonderland

By: Ronny Emerson

Copyright Notes

Table of Contents

Introduction

Have you imagined yourself falling into the magical Wonderland hole with peculiar exotic creatures? Have you been so immersed in Alice's adventures in Wonderland and wish for a bit for yourself? Would you like to embark on an adventure yourself and are clueless about going about it? Are you feeling bored?

Well, you are in the right place, reading the right book. We will bring you your unique adventures. Follow the talking rabbit (this book). Fall into the rabbit hole of Alice's culinary adventure. Follow us through the pages of this book.

In this book, you will learn the essentials of delicious cooking meals. You will become accustomed to making various meals in this recipe book. We will help you master the crucial techniques in cooking. It does not matter if you are a pro or a beginner; there is a new skill to be learned.

Not only will you learn how to make new meals, but you will also build your confidence from the easy-to-make recipes to the more difficult ones in this fantasy land. This book lists important meals that can be shared with loved ones at all times.

We have three different cake recipes to cater to all occasions. We have easy-to-make cupcake recipes for outings, lemon, and an unbirthday cake for birthdays and anniversaries. We also included a wide array of exciting recipes for your parties and events.

Do you have a child that loves Wonderland? Throw her a picture-perfect Alice in the Wonderland-themed party. Your little one will be thrilled.

We decided to write this book because of Alice fans like myself. We could not find a cookbook dedicated to recipes from the book when we needed ideas for an Alice in the Wonderland-themed party. We hope this book will be as important to you as it is to us.

What are you waiting for? Dive in! Let us get cooking. You have all it takes to pull off the meals in this book. Each meal will leave you salivating.

1. Sugar Cookies

Alice ate some strange cookies that appeared out of nowhere after drinking the "drink me" part, hoping that she would shrink back to her adorable petite size. We bring you the best sugar cookies recipe.

Cooking time: thirty minutes

Serving size: 24

List of ingredients:

For sugar cookies

- Two cups of sugar (white)
- One and a half cups of buttered (unsalted and softened)
- One teaspoon of vanilla extracts
- Four eggs
- One teaspoon of salt
- Five cups of flour (all-purpose)
- One tablespoon of baking powder

For sugar cookie frosting

- Three cups of powdered sugar
- One and a half tablespoons of milk
- One cup of softened unsalted butter
- A pinch of salt
- One tablespoon of vanilla extract
- A quarter of a teaspoon of almond extracts
- Frosting coloring

Cooking Instructions

Sugar cookie recipe

Cream the butter and sugar together for the sugar cookie.

Add the vanilla and eggs.

Sieve in the baking powder and flour. Cover the sugar cookie dough for an hour after mixing in the sugar and butter.

Preheat your oven to 400°

Roll your sugar cookie dough into half an inch thickness. Using your cookie cutter, cut into various shapes.

Bake for ten minutes in the oven. Remove and allow to cool.

Sugar cookie frosting recipe

Use a mixer set on low speed; mix the butter and half of the powdered sugar.

When it is well combined, add the rest of the powdered sugar with the mixer speed set at high.

Add the extracts, salt, and milk. Mix for the sugar cookie frosting for thirty seconds. Add proper food coloring to various parts.

You can add powdered sugar to thicken the frosting or liquid milk to reduce the frosting.

2. Drink Me Potion

Poor Alice falls down a rabbit hole, and she decided to drink the potion with "drink me" attached to it. Perhaps not the best decision, but we bring you the potion's recipe.

Cooking time: ten minutes

Serving size: twelve servings

List of ingredients:

- Twelve potion bottles
- Four cups of cranberry juice
- One cup of orange juice
- One cup of pineapple juice
- Two tablespoons of lime juice
- Two cups of ginger ale

Cooking Instructions

Mix the juice in a large bowl.

Refrigerate for at least one hour. Pour the potion bottles.

Attach the drink me tag to it.

3. Butterfly Bread

Little butterfly slices of bread flew in the garden. While we cannot make real-life butterflies with bread wings, the next best thing is a butterfly-shaped bread recipe.

Cooking time: twenty minutes

Serving size: twelve

List of ingredients:

- A quarter of a cup of butter
- One cup of milk
- A half-cup of water
- Five cups of flour (all-purpose)
- One and a half teaspoons of yeast
- One egg
- One and a half teaspoons of salt
- Two tablespoons of sugar

Cooking Instructions

Heat the butter, milk, and water till it is warm.

Mix the dry ingredients. Make a pit in the middle of the dry ingredients and knead for close to eight minutes to make the butterfly bread elastic and smooth.

Oil the butterfly-shaped pans and dust lightly with flour.

Fill the butterfly-shaped pan halfway.

Cover up the pan for thirty-five minutes.

Preheat your oven to 400°

Bake in the oven for fifteen minutes.

4. Little Oysters In The Shell

Curious little oysters were defeated and eaten in the absence of their mama. Here is how the poor oysters were cooked.

Cooking time: ten minutes

Serving size: three servings

List of ingredients:

- Twelve oysters
- Preferred sauce
- Two tablespoons of unsalted butter
- Lemon wedges

Cooking Instructions

Rinse your oysters in cold water. Discard oysters with open shells that do not close when you try to close them.

Fire up your grill to medium-high.

Place your oysters on a grill (cupped side down).

Grill for five minutes for small oysters and eight minutes for large oysters.

Gently remove the oysters from the grill with tongs.

Run a knife along the oyster's inner bottom shell rim to remove the oyster.

Serve the oysters hot with a side of melted butter, lemon wedges, and sauce.

5. Mushroom

Alice ate a mushroom on the advice of a caterpillar. Mushrooms handled Alice's growth. Here is our favorite grow-enhancing mushroom recipe.

Cooking time: eight minutes

Serving size: four

List of ingredients:

- Two tablespoons of butter
- A quarter cup of white wine
- One tablespoon of soy sauce
- One sprig of thyme
- Two tablespoons of olive oil
- Two cloves of minced garlic
- Two cups of mushroom
- Chives to garnish the mushroom

Cooking Instructions

Gently clean the mushroom with paper towels.

Slice into half an inch pieces.

Mix the mushroom and soy sauce.

Heat the butter and oil on high heat, add the mushroom to the sauce. Cook for four minutes before stirring.

Add the thyme and garlic to the mushroom. Give it an occasional stir as you cook for three more minutes. Season with pepper and salt. Remove from heat and serve.

6. Candied Pecans

Candies are essential in Wonderland. We bring you the best-candied pecans recipe from Wonderland.

Cooking time: one hour

Serving size: ten

List of ingredients:

- One cup of sugar
- One egg white
- One teaspoon of cinnamon (ground)
- Two cups of pecans
- One teaspoon of salt
- One tablespoon of water

Cooking Instructions

Mix the cinnamon, salt, and sugar.

Whisk the water and egg white until it froths.

Pour the pecans into the frothy mixture.

Add in the pecans until evenly coated.

Put the coated pecans on a baking sheet and bake in a preheated oven of 250°F for about an hour.

Turn the pecans around in the oven every fifteen minutes.

7. Ice Cream

What is an Alice themed-party without ice cream and colorful sprinkles? Follow our recipe to make the best Alice ice cream.

Cooking time: ten minutes

Serving size: five

List of ingredients:

- One cup of heavy whipping cream
- Two teaspoons of vanilla extracts
- Three-quarter of a cup of sugar (white)
- Two and a quarter cups of liquid milk
- Sprinklers

Cooking Instructions

Over low heat, mix milk, sugar, and cream. Mix until the sugar completely dissolves.

Pour the mixture into a cup and refrigerate overnight.

Mix the ice cream in an ice cream mixer for twenty minutes.

Put the vanilla ice cream in a bowl in the freezer for three hours.

Scoop out and add some sprinkles to it.

8. Cherry Tarts

Alice claims the drink me part tastes like cherry tarts at first. Since we lack the power to bring you cherry tarts as a drink, how about you enjoy these bite-size cherry tarts. We have the perfect recipe for s cherry tart for it.

Cooking time: thirty minutes

Serving size: twelve

List of ingredients:

shell

- A half-cup of sugar
- One large egg
- One and a half cups of flour (all-purpose)
- Eight tablespoons of butter
- One teaspoon of vanilla extracts

Filling

- One cup of sugar
- A quarter of a cup of cornstarch
- Four cups of pitted red cherries

Cooking Instructions

Shell

Mix the all-purpose flour and salt.

Cream the sugar and butter. Add in the vanilla and whisked egg.

Add the all-purpose flour mixture and mix thoroughly.

Flatten the dough till it is one-eighth of an inch thick.

Cut with a round cutter and press each into a muffin tin.

Preheat your oven to 350°

Bake the shells in the oven for twelve minutes.

You can keep the unbaked shells in the refrigerator for up to a month.

Filling

Heat the cherries over medium heat for ten minutes while stirring often.

Whisk the cornstarch and sugar until smooth. Pour in the cherries and mix over low heat.

Let the cherry pie filling simmer for two minutes.

Remove the cherry pie filling from heat when it thickens.

Pour into the tart shell.

You can keep the filled cherry tart for up to twenty-four hours.

9. Edible Plates

Mad hatter dipped his saucer in tea and took a bite out of it. What could be more exciting than an edible plate? It will be an absolute favorite at any gathering. Follow our recipe to make delicious edible plates.

Cooking time: fifteen minutes

Serving size: four

List of ingredients:

- White chocolate
- Plate molds
- Food coloring (optional)

Cooking Instructions

Melt the white chocolate in a hot water bath.

Fill the plate molds with chocolate.

Allow setting for thirty minutes.

Carefully remove the white chocolate plates from the molds.

10. Cupcakes

Take a cupcake for the road, perhaps. Follow our fantastic recipe to make delicious cupcakes.

Cooking time: twenty-five minutes

Serving size: twelve

List of ingredients:

- One and a quarter teaspoons of baking soda
- Three-quarter of a cup of sugar
- One and a quarter of a cup of flour (all-purpose)
- Half a cup of softened butter (unsalted)
- A half teaspoon of salt
- Two large eggs
- A half-cup of buttermilk
- Two teaspoons of vanilla extracts

Cooking Instructions

Mix the dry ingredients for the cupcake.

Cream the butter and sugar at medium for up to five minutes.

Fold in the dry ingredient.

Preheat your oven to 350°

Line the cupcake pan with a cupcake liner each.

Fill twelve cupcake liners two-third.

Bake for twenty to twenty-five minutes (put a toothpick in the center of each cupcake, if it comes out clean, it is done).

Pipe frosting onto each cupcake and press some sprinkles into it.

11. Roast Turkey

The last taste Alice's potion has is like roast turkey. We lack the superpowers to bring you roast turkey in liquid form, but I bet roast turkey tastes as good as the liquid one. Try out our easy-to-make recipe.

Cooking time: four hours

Serving size: twenty

List of ingredients:

- One large turkey (feet and innards removed)
- A half-cup of butter(unsalted)
- Two cups of kosher salt
- Two large peeled onion
- Four stalks of celery
- Four carrots stick (chopped)
- One bay leaf
- Two sprigs of thyme
- One cup of dry wine (wine)

Cooking Instructions

Rub kosher salt all over the turkey. Add some inside it.

Place the salted turkey in a bowl of cold water, covering it. Refrigerate the salted turkey in water overnight.

Preheat your oven to 350°F.

Remove the turkey from the salty water and rinse in clean water.

Melt the butter and brush it over the turkey. Stuff the turkey with half of the vegetables. Put the remaining around the tray. Place the turkey with the breast side down in the roasting tray. Pour the white wine over it.

Turn the turkey to its sides in the oven every ninety minutes. Grill in the oven for four hours or until the internal temperature of 180°F.

Remove the turkey from the grill, brush the remaining butter on the turkey. Your turkey is ready to be carved.

Serve the carved turkey bits.

12. Hot Buttered Toast

The potion also tastes like hot buttered toast. How about you follow our recipe to make the perfect hot buttered toast you will ever have.

Cooking time: ten minutes

Serving size: three servings

List of ingredients:

- Six slices of bread
- Six dollops of butter

Cooking Instructions

Heat the toaster, pop your slice of bread inside it one at a time till the timer goes off.

Put a dollop of butter on hot toast bread and serve hot.

13. Pops

Cold peaches pop for a hot afternoon sounds like a great idea in Wonderland. Enjoy your popsicles

Cooking time: fifteen

Serving size: eight

List of ingredients:

- One and a half cups of yogurt (Greek)
- A quarter of a teaspoon of cinnamon
- One cup of granola without raisins
- Two teaspoons of brown sugar
- Eight paper cups or pop molds
- Two cups of sliced peaches (drained)
- A pinch of nutmeg

Cooking Instructions

Mix the Greek yogurt, nutmeg, granola, and cinnamon.

Add a layer of yogurt into the eight pop molds paper cups, followed by the peaches. Continue the layering till you exhaust the ingredients.

Stick a pops stick into the paper cups or pop mold.

Freeze until the pop hardens.

14. Custard

A little bowl of custard and some fruits to adorn its edges makes the potion perfect, don't you agree? Follow this recipe for a custard you will always love.

Cooking time: ten minutes

Serving size: eight

List of ingredients:

- One tablespoon of vanilla extracts
- Four eggs
- Four cups of milk (whole)
- Three tablespoons of cornstarch
- One teaspoon of butter
- Sugar/maple syrup/honey
- Fruits for garnishing

Cooking Instructions

Over medium heat, boil the vanilla extracts, butter, and milk.

In another bowl, mix the cornstarch, egg, and sugar until the sugar dissolves fully.

Reduce the heat to low, add the egg and cornstarch mixture slowly to the milk.

Continue stirring until the custard thickens; this takes less than ten minutes.

Allow cooling before garnishing with fruits. Add more sweetener if need be.

15. Pineapple Smoothie

A pineapple-tasting potion seems like a great way to start the day. Join us for a refreshing cup of pineapple smoothie.

Cooking time: five minutes

Serving size: two

List of ingredients:

- Two cups of chopped pineapple
- A half-cup of coconut water
- A half-cup of yogurt
- Two cups of ice
- Pineapple wedge for garnishing

Cooking Instructions

Mix all ingredients except ice and blend.

Add the crushed ice to it. Serve immediately with pineapple wedge as garnish.

16. Unbirthday Cake

It might look like a birthday cake, have birthday candles, but I promise you it is not. We hope you will enjoy baking an unbirthday cake with this recipe.

Cooking time: two hours

Serving size: twelve

List of ingredients:

For cake

- two eggs
- a half cup of butter
- one cup of sugar (white)
- one and a half cups of flour (multipurpose)
- a half cup of milk
- two teaspoons of vanilla extracts

For frosting

- Four teaspoons of milk
- Six cups of sugar (powdered)
- Three teaspoons of vanilla
- Three-quarter of a cup of softened butter
- Cake sprinkles

Cooking Instructions

To make the cake

Cream the sugar and butter till it is well mixed.

Add in the eggs, one at a time. Add the vanilla extracts and flour. Fold in until the cake batter is well mixed.

Preheat the oven to 350°F, grease your cake pan, then lightly dust with flour.

Bake in a nine by nine-inch pan for twenty minutes. If a small knife is put in the middle of it comes out clean. Your cake is made.

To make frosting

Mix the butter and sugar on your electric mixer at low speed.

Add a tablespoon of milk at a time. If the white cake frosting is too thick, add the remaining frosting.

Divide the cake into two equal sizes and layer it with frosting.

Put on a cake board and apply frosting—Press multicolored sprinklers around the cake.

Add the candles to the cake.

17. Magic Wand

Wonderland is crawling with magic, and a little girl needs a magic wand to fight hunger and conjure items. Here is how to make perfectly edible and colorful wands.

Cooking time: thirty minutes

Serving size: twenty

List of ingredients:

- Twenty pretzels rod
- Two cups of white chocolate chips
- Colored sugar
- Sprinklers
- Food glitters

Cooking Instructions

You can melt the chocolate simply by placing it in a microwave for one minute, remove it from the microwave, and stir.

Return the white chocolate to the microwave for thirty seconds, remove and stir. Continue to repeat this method until the chocolate is fully melted.

Dip one end of the pretzels in the chocolate, add some sprinkles on it or glitters or color sugar.

Allow the chocolate to set.

Serve immediately.

18. Sour Cream

A garden party cannot be complete without a good dip. You can always count on easy-to-make sour cream for all snacks that needs a dip. Follow our recipe to make original sour cream.

Cooking time: four minutes

Serving size: twelve

List of ingredients:

- Two tablespoons of onion (dried)
- Two cups of sour cream
- One tablespoon of parsley (chopped)
- Two teaspoons of garlic powder
- One teaspoon of paprika
- One teaspoon of dry mustard
- Salt to taste

Cooking instructions:

Mix all the ingredients.

Allow cooling in the refrigerator for two hours before serving.

19. Potato Chips

Sour cream goes well with potato chips. Make your healthy low salt chips with our recipe.

Cooking time: 20 minutes

Serving size: eight

List of ingredients:

- Four medium-sized potatoes
- Oil
- Three tablespoons of salt

Cooking instructions:

Peel and slice your potato into paper-thin size.

As you slice, put it in a bowl of cold water. Drain the water when you finish slicing.

Add cold water to cover up the potatoes and add salt to the water. Leave it for 20 minutes.

On high heat, heat your oil in a deep fryer to 365°F. Fry your potatoes in small quantities until you are done frying. You can also use an air-fryer for a healthier meal.

Put the fried golden potatoes on a paper towel to absorb all excess oil. Serve when cool.

20. Chocolate Tea

Mad hatter had a cup of tea which he ended up putting his plate inside. Here is how to make the perfect tea for your tea party.

Cooking time: Five minutes

Serving size: three

List of ingredients:

- Two cups of water
- Three teaspoons of dark cocoa powder
- Four tablespoons of sweetened chocolate
- Two teabags
- A half-cup of milk
- Two tablespoons of brown sugar

Cooking Instructions

Put the teabags into the water and boil.

Add the other ingredients. Let it boil for five minutes.

Remove the teabags and serve immediately.

Add a teaspoon of cinnamon to the tea for a spicy feel.

21. Goat Cheese

Goat cheese is a staple in every tea party. Find out how to make party-hit goat cheese.

Cooking time: 40 minutes

Serving: eight

Ingredient list:

- Eight and the third cup of fresh goat's milk
- One teaspoon of kosher salt (cheese salt)
- One tablespoon of lime juice

Cooking instruction:

Pour your goat milk into a large pot.

Add the lemon juice to the milk and mix.

Heat the milk till it reaches 185°F.

Remove the milk from the fire, cover it up and allow it to sit for ten minutes.

Put a cheese close on a sieve and pour the milk mixture into it. Allow the goat cheese to drain for 60 minutes.

Add kosher salt to your drained goat cheese and mix thoroughly.

Roll the cheese into a rod-like shape using plastic wrap or put it in a mold.

Secure the ends of the plastic wraps by twisting the edges before placing them in the fridge to set.

22. Cherry Jam

Cherry jam is a perfect alternative for those who prefer jam and not butter on their hot buttered toast. We have the perfect recipe below.

Cooking time: 50 minutes

Serving size: thirty

List of ingredients:

- 1.5kg of your preferred fruit (cherry)
- Three cups of sugar
- Two tablespoons of lemon juice
- A quarter of a teaspoon of salt

Cooking Instructions

Cut the fruit into one-inch chunks.

Mix the sugar, salt, and fruit on medium heat. When it boils for three minutes and the sugar is wholly dissolved, mash the fruit using a potato masher.

Add lemon juice to the mashed mixture while boiling until the bubbles reduce on low heat for about six minutes to set.

Scoop the jam into sterilized jam bottles while it is still hot. Close the cap. The fruit jam will thicken as it cools down.

The jam can be stored in a cupboard for up to six months.

23. Mini Sandwich

A perfectly made mini sandwich is needed to go with the tea at the tea party. You can make cute little mini sandwiches by following the instructions below.

Cooking time: five

Serving size: four

List of ingredients:

- Four slices of bread
- Four tablespoons of mustard
- Four slices of ham
- Four tablespoons of cream cheese
- Four teaspoons of cheddar cheese
- Two leaves of romaine lettuce
- Four toothpicks

Cooking Instructions

Spread the mustard on each of the two slices of bread; put a slice of ham on the two slices of bread.

Follow with cream cheese on one slice of bread and cedar cheese on the other. Place a leaf of romaine lettuce on one of the bread slices. Cover up with the other prepared slice of bread. Repeat for the other two slices.

Pile the two sandwiches on each other. Stick four toothpicks in the piled sandwich.

Cut into four.

24. Edible Stone

In Wonderland, not only plates are edible, but stones are too. Make perfectly edible stones with this recipe.

Cooking time: thirty minutes

Serving size: ten

List of ingredients:

- One kilogram of white chocolate
- One kilogram of milk chocolate
- One kilogram of dark chocolate

Cooking Instructions

Melt the chocolate in different containers in boiling water.

Pour the melted chocolate into your stone mold.

Let it set for about forty minutes.

25. Chocolate Chips Cookies

On the garden table were some delicious-looking cookies. Adorn your garden table with some of yours with this easy recipe.

Cooking time: thirty minutes

Serving size: twenty

List of ingredients:

- One cup of softened butter
- Two cups of brown sugar
- Two teaspoons of vanilla extracts
- Two large eggs
- Two teaspoons of water(hot)
- One teaspoon of baking soda
- A half teaspoon of salt
- Two cups of chocolate chips
- Three cups of all-purpose flour
- One cup of walnut (chopped)

Cooking Instructions

Mix the sugar, butter until it is smooth. Add your beaten egg and vanilla to the mix and stir.

Dissolve your salt and baking powder in hot water. Add to the butter mixture.

Sieve in the flour, fold in the chocolate chips and nuts.

Preheat your oven to 350°F. Using a big spoon, drop a scoop into an ungreased baking pan.

Bake for twelve minutes until the edges are brown.

Allow cooling before serving.

26. Lemon Cake

What cake resembles sunlight and happiness? I know, it is the lemon cake. Why not follow our recipe to create happiness and sunlight where you are?

Cooking time: 23 minutes

Serving: five

Ingredient list:

- A quarter cup of sugar
- One tablespoon of honey
- Three tablespoons of butter
- Three yolks of egg
- One lemon zest
- A quarter teaspoon of salt, mace, and clover
- A half teaspoon of baking soda
- One and a quarter cup of all-purpose flour (sifted)

Cooking instruction:

Cream your premeasured sugar and butter together till it is smooth.

Mix your egg yolk. Add baking soda, spice, zest, and salt.

Gently fold the flour into the mixture until a smooth dough is formed.

Shape the dough into a big cycle.

Preheat your oven to 300°F. Bake the lemon cake for 15 minutes in an oven.

Leave to cool down on a wire rack.

Divide the cake into two, add frosting in between the layer.

Pipe some frosting over it to create the perfect cake.

27. Pudding

It must be some pudding for a butterfly bread to chastise Alice for being impertinent. Learn how to make the perfect pudding below.

Cooking time: forty minutes

Serving size: Four

List of ingredients:

- Two eggs
- Nine tablespoons of granulated sugar
- Five tablespoons of hot water
- 250ml of milk
- Four cups of custard
- Unsalted butter

Cooking Instructions

Coat four the pudding cups with butter.

Put four tablespoons of sugar and three tablespoons of water in a pan on medium-high heat.

Stir the sugar and water mixture until the sugar dissolves completely in the water, and the fluid becomes a golden brown mixture. Stir it and remove it from heat. Add two teaspoons of hot water to the caramel.

Divide the caramel into the prepared pudding cups.

Boil the milk and sugar in a pot. Beat the eggs until it foams lightly.

Add the hot milk and sugar to the egg while mixing it.

Divide the egg and milk into the pudding cup with caramel.

Cover each of the custards with aluminum foil to prevent the pudding from being dry and allow for even cooking of the pudding.

Put a pan of water on medium, place the pudding gently into the pan, and cover.

Reduce the heat under the pudding to low and boil for twenty minutes. Ensure the water is not at boiling temperature as the pudding steams.

Remove the pudding from the fire.

Tip your pudding onto a plate by running a knife around the edge of a cup.

Your pudding is ready to be enjoyed.

28. Fruit Salad

Wonderland is filled with lots of fruits that will make the best fruit salads. Treat yourself to a wonderland fruit salad.

Cooking time: thirty minutes

Serving size: ten

List of ingredients:

- Two cups of diced pineapples
- Two cups of strawberries sliced in half
- Two cups of blueberries
- Two cups of sliced kiwi
- Two cups of grapes
- One peeled orange

Cooking Instructions

Mix all fruits in a bowl, as shown above.

Refrigerate for at least thirty minutes or until you are ready to serve.

29. Herb's Eggs

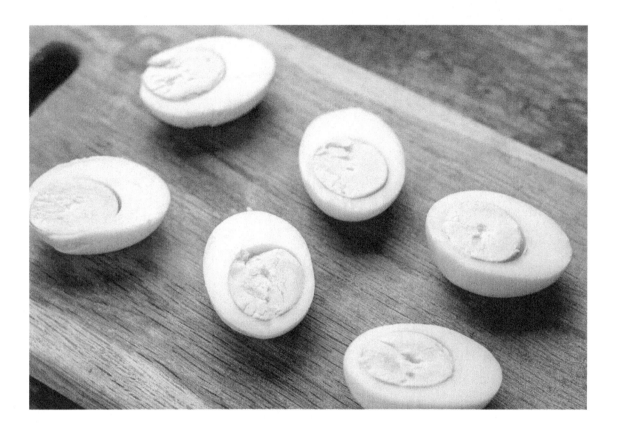

Alice believes Humpty Dumpty looks like an egg even though Humpty disagrees. Here is how to make colorful eggs that look just like Humpty.

Cooking time: Thirty minutes

Serving size: twelve

List of ingredients:

- A small bag of onion peels
- Twelve eggs
- Turmeric
- Cilantro
- Parsley
- Red cabbage
- Rubber bands
- Mason jars
- Old stockings

Cooking Instructions

Hard boil the eggs.

Mix three tablespoons of turmeric with three cups of water. Boil for twenty minutes on high heat for the yellow color.

Two cups of diced red cabbage boiled with two cups of water for twenty minutes for blue color. Or use onion skin for orange color using the same process.

Lay cilantro or parsley leaves on the side of an egg. Put it inside a cut piece of leg stocking.

Secure the end of the stocking with a rubber band or tie a knot.

Drain the water from the dyes into a mason jar.

Divide the eggs into the dye mason jars. Cover up for twenty-four hours.

Remove the eggs after a day, remove the stocking and leaf to reveal a beautiful pattern in the colored leaves.

30. Meringues

We will complete our cookbook with beautifully colored meringues. Don't just admire the pictures; make some of your own with our recipe.

Cooking time: One hour

Serving size: thirty

List of ingredients:

- A half teaspoon of cream of tartar
- One cup of granulated sugar
- Four large eggs white
- One teaspoon of vanilla extract
- Multiple gel food coloring

Cooking Instructions

With your mixer on medium speed, beat your egg white till it is entirely foamy.

Stop the mixer and add your cream and continue mixing until the mixture turns to opaque white.

Add a spoonful of sugar at a time, continue mixing with your mixer until it is thoroughly mixed.

Stop the mixer when the mixture is stiff. Add the vanilla extracts at this point.

Divide the meringues and add different colors by stirring the meringues gently to incorporate the color.

Preheat your oven to 200° Line the baking tray with baking paper.

Put the meringues in a piping bag and pipe them onto the parchment paper.

Bake in the oven for sixty minutes.

Conclusion

Dear Wonderland adventurers, thank you for coming this far with us. Alice in Wonderland was written by a mathematician who managed to bring in so many "variables," as they say in mathematics. He created a book so perfect, beyond anyone's imagination at the time it was written. Nothing close to it has ever been written, and for that creative genius, we are forever grateful.

Wonderland tells us everything is possible, and we can experience magic if only we are willing to open our minds to it. The author's life has shown beyond a shred of doubt that the only limitations that exist are within us. Let go of your inhibitions, loosen up, set yourself free of doubts, and take life by a storm.

You might be talked about years after you have passed. While achieving these dreams, continue to create your own fantasy with our Alice in Wonderland-themed book. We cannot wait to hear of your exploits.

Author's Afterthoughts

The fact that you all have read this book means more than you know. However, I've seen how much feedback has helped me grow in the last few years. Those comments on things that I have unintentionally overlooked make me go back to the drawing board. I would love you to leave some feedback as well. This will be useful in making sure I churn out high-quality books for you all the time. Also, it doesn't hurt that your feedback will help guide those searching for the right book.

Thanks,

Ronny Emerson

About the Author

Ronny Emerson is mostly referred to as magic fingers. He has the unique ability to create the best dishes out of ordinary ingredients. This skilled culinary professional is recognized for his contributions to the creation of exceptional gastronomic delights. After he won his first cooking contest at 9, there was nowhere else to go but up. His father has always been his role model for cooking tasty dishes. It was under his tutelage that he grew to become the professional we know today.

Ronny travels around the world, where he samples different cuisine from diverse cultures. He cherishes the opportunity to enjoy the various flavors from these restaurants. With what he has learned on his travels, Ronny heads home to his base in New York, where he makes his unique recipes with a brilliant blend of these cultures. So far, he has found comfort in working for one of the top restaurants in the city as the executive chef. Ronny also loves to share what he comes up with in the kitchen.

Made in the USA
Monee, IL
27 November 2021

83156403R00044